# Introduction

Debt, for some, is a constant source of anxiety and stress, for others it has simply become so prevalent in their lives that they cannot even imagine themselves not having it. Debt can range from small and manageable to large and overwhelming; wherever you fall on the spectrum this is the eBook for you. It is almost impossible to not obtain some sort of debt during the course of a lifetime, whether it is student loans, a mortgage or credit card debt, it is something the vast majority of humanity will experience in some form. So often, lives are ruined because of poor money management decisions, before it gets to that point it is imperative that you learn the tools necessary to improve your situation. This eBook will give you the tools to manage your debt or get out of it completely!

The word debt has such a negative connotation that many of us can't imagine there being such a thing as good debt. Many are definitely not able to differentiate between good and bad debt. This eBook will go into detail on this topic so that you will be able to make a clear distinction between the different types of debt and identify them in your own life. Another topic this eBook will cover a the reasons one should get out of bad debt and of course how to get out of it. Another topic that will be covered is knowing if and when one should file for bankruptcy and many more. These chapters will assist those who feel stuck in their current situation by giving them the information and tools required for them to take the first steps to improve their situation, however grim they feel it is.

Reading this eBook will give you new hope, and hopefully get you out of the constraints of debt and living freely again. The decisions we make regarding debt could make a large difference in the quality of our lives. So wait no more, it's about time that you stop allowing your debt to control you, it's time for you to take over the reins and learn how to become debt free for good.

# Disclaimer

This book is intended to be a general guide, to raise awareness, and to help people make informed decisions in the context of their own person circumstance.

As everybody's circumstances are different, so are the actions you should take. While many of the strategies in this book can be applied by almost anybody regardless of which country they live in, each country has its own law with regards to issues such as bankruptcy. Therefore, it is best to speak to a lawyer before you make some of the major decisions outlined in this book.

The author accepts no responsibility for any loss, be it personal or financial, as a result for the use or misuse of the information in this book.

If you have any doubts or concerns after reading this book, please speak to a financial advisor or other qualified person before making any firm decisions.

# **Contents**

## **Chapter 1**
The Difference between Good
Debt and Bad Debt

## **Chapter 2**
6 Reasons Why You Should
Get Out of Bad Debt

## **Chapter 3**
13 Step Simple Bad Debt Busting Strategy

## **Chapter 4**
Should You Consolidate Your Debt or Declare
Bankruptcy?

## **Chapter 5**
How to Live Debt Free

# Chapter 1

## The Difference between Good Debt and Bad Debt

While most people can live one hundred percent debt-free, depending on your personal circumstances it's not always the smartest thing to do. Most people cannot earn enough money to pay cash for life's most important purchases, like a new car or a house. It is most important that before you sign on the dotted line for a loan or buy credit, that you know whether the loan you're considering on taking is for good debt or bad debt.

Good debt is money borrowed on an investment that over time will make you money, or at the very least save you money (i.e., an *asset*; one borrows money to purchase a positively geared rental property). Yes, there is a certain level of risk, but if you invest wisely and have a good real estate agent, you can lower these risks. By having a rental as an asset, tenants will pay the debt for you and eventually when the house is paid, your tenants will be providing you with positive income-- money you DON'T have to work for after the debt is paid. Ideally, your home would increase in value over that time, which would cancel out any unforeseen expenses which may occur.

Many people consider taking out a mortgage to also be a form of good debt, and these same people will tell you that "your home is your greatest asset." Generally, I beg to differ and while it is not the best example of bad debt I still consider it to be bad debt and here is why. While it is true that we all need a place to call home, most people cannot afford to buy a home in cash. Though, for most people there is a sense of security in one day paying off their mortgage and never having to worry about rent. However, remember that interest and bank fees on the mortgage as well as property maintenance are always taking money out of your pocket. In most parts of the world houses attract some form of property tax or tax you have to pay to occupy the property. Many countries have different names for it, such as in Australia where they are called "rates", but regardless of the name, it is still tax- which takes money out of your pocket. This then make your personal home a financial *liability* rather than an asset.

Another and even better example of bad debt would be a car loan. Generally, car loans attract higher interest than mortgages, but like a mortgage, the interest is money leaving your pocket. Most cars are guaranteed to lose value every year; there is also the cost of maintenance to consider, as well as all the other expenses of owning a motor vehicle.

We are always told that your home and car are your greatest assets, but this is not completely true.

For example, the home in which you are living in and paying off is an asset to the financial institution who legally own the property until you pay it off because they will continue to collect interest and fees until the property is completely paid. In the case of property tax, it is also an asset to the state as they will continue to collect tax from you as long as the property is under your name.

Bad debt is debt incurred on purchase that does not generate any long term income. This also includes anything that loses value overtime. When you are paying off bad debt, you are just lining somebody else's pocket for money that they loaned you for something which you will not see any long term financial gain on.

So yes, a personal home loan or car loan is an asset for financial institution you owe money to and are paying interest to.

Simply put, an asset is something that puts money is the owners pocket over time and a liability is something that takes money out.

An exception is a mortgage. Since people cannot afford to pay cash for a house, the easiest rule to follow is if you cannot afford to pay cash for it, don't badly need it, then don't borrow or buy it.

If you buy the newest, fanciest mobile phone on credit for $400 using your credit card and cannot repay the balance of your credit card for a very long time, that mobile phone may cost you over $500 dollars and by then the mobile phone will be out of style, out dated and will be worth next to nothing.

Cash advance loans or Payday loans are among the worst kinds of debt. With a Payday loan, the lender writes a personal check to the borrower for the amount the borrower would like to borrow, plus a fee. The borrower then has until their next payday to pay back the loan, plus the fee and any interest incur over that period of time. If the borrower cannot pay the loan by their next payday, they will incur yet more processing fees to roll over the loan. The interest on these types of loans can be huge, starting at an annual rate of 300%. These types of loans are almost a modern and legal form of loan sharking.

It is worth keeping all of the above in mind before considering a taking a loan.

# Chapter 2

## 6 Reasons Why You Should Get Out Of Bad Debt

### 1.    It Will Free Up Your Household Income

Would you like a pay raise?

Think of all the money you are spending on interest repayments, bank fees, and other charges associated with servicing your debt, be it a credit card, car loan or mortgage.

That's real cash you could use to reinvest or make more money or buy life's luxury with cash and enjoy them with a piece of mind.

## 2. Less Stress in Your Life

When you have debt it is an extra burden.

How would you feel if for whatever reason you lost your job tomorrow?

Would you be worried that the car, home, or any other belonging you have will soon be repossessed?

Did you know that most domestic relationship break down due to financial disagreements?

One of the best ways to live a less stressful, more for filling life is to eliminate negative financial obligations.

## 3. You Will Be More Motivated to Achieve Your Long-Term Financial Objectives.

Fact: For many people there is nothing more soul sucking than going to work to earn money to pay for something they cannot benefit from, like interest repayments; or having to go to work because they know that if they don't and cannot afford the repayment, they'll lose everything.

People who don't have these financial troubles usually are more positively motivated, which means they will usually work harder doing work that they find more enjoyable because they have more freedom to choose the occupation that they find more enjoyable rather than work out of desperation. The people without financial troubles are able to save or invest for their long term objectives their time is more productively spent doing things which they are more likely to gain from.

## 4. It Will Improve Your Health.

Healthier mind equals healthier body. It has been proven the lower your stress levels, the lower your chances of developing many of the ailments related to stress such as mental illness and heart disease.

Being debt free will, at the very least, remove one source of stress from your life.

## 5.  Unfortunate Events are Less Likely to Ruin Your Financial and/or Personal Life.

Fact: When you owe any bank or financial institution money, in most parts of the world, they can take any property of value equal to the money owed. This means if you suddenly lose your job or are ill and cannot work, unless you can come up with the money to cover your repayments, then you have a greater chance of losing everything.

If you are debt free or have good debt you may have savings or investments, which means you will be in a better financial position should the unthinkable happen.

## 6. There Is No Better Feeling Than Knowing You Own Something Out Right.

Nothing feels better than the feeling of having paid your debt and knowing you no longer have to worry about the repayments any more. Better yet, buying something in cash and knowing you are free to enjoy what you purchase without ever having to worry about a repayment, interest rates or repossession.

# Chapter 3

# 13 Step Bad Debt Busting Strategy

Unfortunately it is often easier to get into debt than it is to get out, which is why I have formulated this proven easy to follow plan. If properly followed, it can help most people overcome their debt induced financial trouble.

## 1.   Acknowledge You Have a Problem

The first thing you need to do is acknowledge that you have a problem with debt, you cannot begin to turn things around until you take a good, hard look at yourself and admit there is a problem. All you have to do for the first week is to tell yourself, "I have debt problems, because I spend money I don't have. BUT, I know I can do something about this. I can make a plan, control my spending habits and eventually get out of debt."

If you can do this alone, it's a huge step in the right direction. Now set a day once a week where you can spend just 45 minutes to one hour dealing with your financial situation and make sure you don't miss this appointment.

## 2.  See If You Can Stop Buying Non-Essential Items

When you're in a financial hole the first thing you need to do is stop digging and that's exactly what you will be doing on the second week. For the next 30 days, see if you can stop buying non-essential items. If your major problem is credit card, NOW is the time to grab some sharp scissors and cut them you, believe me you will never need it again. If your main problem is not a credit card, at the very least put them away and don't use them to pay for any non- essential items for at least this 30 day period.

After this 30 day period you can decide how much you want to spend on non-essential items.

## 3.  Make Small Cost Reductions

On the third week, review what you normally buy and try to cut a few off them, or at least spend less money on them. If you need to buy food, see if you can buy generic brands rather than name brands. Have a coffee at home or pack a Thermos, rather than buying one at a shop. Try packing a lunch to work instead of buying from the shops or canteen.

If you follow step 2 & 3 with dedication you may be surprised at how the savings start piling up.

## 4.  Set Up an Emergency Account

On the fourth week, you are going to set up a saving account if you don't already have one for an emergency account. Take the amount you've saved by implementing steps 2 and set up an automatic deposit from your checking account to this emergency account. At first, aim for $1000, which you can grow later. The reason for this account is if you are faced with unexpected cost, the money from this account will cover the loan repayments of your debts.

## 5.  Create an Inventory

This is the step most people hate to take. But take a deep breath. You have to do this. Don't forget the determination you had at the first step. This is something you can do. On the fifth week you will set up a spreadsheet. In the first column list all you debts, for example your medical bills, car loan, and credit cards. If you want, you can leave out your mortgage, but make sure you include every other debt. Put the amount of money you owe for each debt in the second column. In the third column, put the minimum monthly repayments. In the fourth column put the percentage of interest. Add up the second and third columns to see the total debt you owe and how much you need to pay, at a minimum, toward the debt every month.

## 6.  Create a Spending Plan

This isn't as painful as it sounds. You are going to set up another spreadsheet this sixth week. In the first column, put down you monthly bills, for example your mortgage/rent, gas, water and electricity- any recurring payment you need to make every month. After you have finished listing these expenses, list all the expenses that change every month, like groceries and dining out. Later on you should add your odd expenses like car repairs, clothes, or licences. But as we want to keep this as simple as possible at the moment we won't get into this now. Put the costs of each in the second column. Make sure you put enough money for items such as food and fuel, because you don't want to get caught short. Make sure to include your minimum debt repayments and emergency account deposit. Finally list your monthly income. Now you should have a monthly spending plan. If your expenses are higher then you income, you will need to make spending adjustments until your expenses are equal or lower than your income.

## 7.  Control Your Spending

If you are into your seventh week of this plan and are finding it difficult to stick to the plan. Here is the most important thing to do. First deposit money into your emergency account. Second, into you debt repayments. Third, into your monthly bills and finally withdraw the variable amount of cash, and place them in separate envelopes. Using this method you don't have to worry about overspending as when the envelopes are empty, you cannot spend any more. Keep gradually cutting back your expenses at this point so you can stick to you spending plan.

## 8. Pay Your Bills on Time

For many people this can be a problem. However if you want to get out of debt you need to start paying your bill in time. If you have follow the payment plan in step 7, you should pay your bills before you get to any discretionary spending items. At this point in time you will want to focus on making it a habit to pay your bills on time. Try these methods if you have trouble remembering: 1) pay bills as soon as they come or 2) add a reminder in your calender program to inform you when the bill are due.

## 9. Start Making Extra Repayments

Remember the quicker you pay these debts off the more financially secure you will be and the more money you will save in recurring interest payments. By now you should know how much debt you owe, should have some money in your emergency account, you should have a spending plan and be paying your bills on time and be able to control your spending. Now you can start focusing on paying down your debt. This is what you need to do if you can find at least $150 worth of savings from your spending plan, use this to start making extra repayments, to do this you may have to cut further back into your discretionary spending. Or as soon as you emergency account reaches $1000, you can start diverting any extra payments toward extra debt repayments. Once you have found that $150 have a look at your debt spreadsheet. Firstly grade the debts from smallest to largest. Now, look at the smallest debt owed and start paying that $150 toward it PLUS the minimum monthly repayment, until the debt is completely paid off.

Now you are going to take that $150 PLUS the minimum repayment of the first debt and use it to pay off the second smallest debt. Repeat this process with every debt you have, gradually paying of the larger debts until they are all paid off. Once these debts are all cleared you will have a fairly substantial amount of money which you can divert into growing your emergency account, funding your infrequent expenses, and eventually start investing.

## 10. Find Bigger Savings

Once you have your finances under control and have started making extra debt repayments, you should look for ways to further cut costs, and increase the speed at which you get out of debt. Look for larger cuts, like can you move to a more affordable house? Can you down size your car to a smaller used model or maybe just get by with one car? Can you cut back on some of the services you're currently using? Whatever savings you can find-- DON'T spend it. Use the extra as repayments on your debts because the quicker you pay each debt off the easier it will get.

## 11.  Expand Your Income

As well as the above mentioned steps another way to pay down your debts faster is to make more money! Any extra cent you can earn over your current income can help. Can you find ways to increase your income? Have a good hard think about this because the possibilities are endless. Maybe you can start a side business in your spare time or a small online business? Get a temporary part-time job. Heck, this problem you now have could be an opportunity in disguise.

## 12.  Keep Tracking Your Progress

Update your spreadsheet every pay day as you pay down your debt. This will help keep you motivated as you can see the debt balance coming down. Your records should be so accurate that you can count down the the time you have left before each debt is completely paid off and will be debt free.

## 13.  Celebrate!

It is important to celebrate as you eliminate each debt. Make this a learning adventure. I can be an amazing feeling to stop wasting money on interest repayments and start gaining financial control of your life. Find ways to have fun and celebrate whilst being frugal and make sure you congratulate yourself each step of the way.

# Chapter 4

## Should You Consolidate Your Debt or Declare Bankruptcy?

In these economic times debt consolidation and declaring bankruptcy have become popular strategies to manage debt and depending on your particular position these are strategies worth considering.

## Debt Consolidation

People often promote consolidation as simple means of saving your money and your credit rating. Consolidation means reorganizing all your debts into one repayment. You may choose consolidate via an unsecured or a secured loan.

## The Advantages & Disadvantages of Debt Consolidation

## The Advantages

### You Can Protect Your Reputation and Credit Rating

If you declare bankruptcy, records of your bankruptcy will be on the public record, which means anyone who looks hard enough will be able to find this out, especially since bankruptcy records are viewable at any federal bankruptcy courthouse. This will lower your credit rating. On the other hand debt consolidation is not a matter of public record and although a consolidation loan may still show up on your credit report, it does not usually lower your credit rating like bankruptcy can.

## You May Still Maintain Your Access to Credit

You may still use your credit card unless specifically prohibited by the agreement of your consolidation loan. However, you may not be approved for credit if you owe a large amount of money or are in default and therefore may not be able to use your credit card. Also, continuing to use your credit card defeats the purpose of consolidating your debts.

## You Can Simplify Your Debt Repayments

With a consolidated loan, you no longer have to worry about keeping up with multiple repayments, or differing interest rates, all you need to do is make one convenient payment.

## Lower Interest Monthly Payment Plans

With a consolidated loan you may be able to reduce the current interest on you repayments and may be able to receive a more flexible payment plan, which can leave you with some spare cash to meet your other financial commitments.

# The Disadvantages

Though there may be some advantages to debt consolidation. It is not a decision to be taken lightly. It may end up costing you money in hidden fees and tax. Most importantly you could end up losing your property.

## You Could End Up Losing Your Property
Anything you use collateral can be seized in the event you cannot meet the repayments, including your home or car.

## You Could End Up Paying More Tax
Depending on your financial situation, any money you may save from debt may be deemed to be income by the tax department, which means you will have to pay tax on it.

# The Advantages and Disadvantages of Declaring Bankruptcy

Through bankruptcy you can restructure or eliminate certain debts while under protection from the federal bankruptcy court. In the US individuals or small businesses commonly file for Chapter 7 and Chapter 13 bankruptcy. Chapter 7 bankruptcies allow the debtor to eliminate many types of debt while a Chapter 13 allows the debtor to restructure their debts and pay their debts via a structured payment plan.

# The Advantages

## You Are Granted Protection from Creditors

Once bankruptcy is granted you will get an automatic stay. An automatic stay will prohibit most creditors or their collectors from trying to collect money from you.

An automatic stay has the power to prevent lawsuits, harassing phone calls, repossessions and foreclosures

## You Can Start Over

Via a Chapter 7 bankruptcy, you can eliminate most of your unsecured debts such as credit cards. You can also surrender any assets you have debts on if you no longer wish to service these debts.

Via a Chapter 13 bankruptcy, you can repay some of your unsecured debts via a supervised payment plan. And depending on your circumstances may be able to save your car or home from being repossessed.

# The Disadvantages

## You Will Have To Sacrifices A Few Luxuries

To qualify for bankruptcy you may have to surrender a few non-essential possessions. If you file for a Chapter 13 bankruptcy you will be placed on as strict budget and without the court's permission you will not be allowed to obtain credit.

## It Will Impact Negatively On Your Credit Rating

A bankruptcy ruling will lower your credit score. Depending on the type of bankruptcy you claim, the claim will remain on your credit report for up to ten years. However, if you have already defaulted on a significant amount of debt this won't make much difference. When you receive your bankruptcy discharge, the bankruptcy issue will be settled and you have a clean slate. Some creditors will ever try to solicit recent bankruptcy debtors because they know a debtor cannot file for bankruptcy again for a certain time.

## Note

The information in this chapter is designed to give you a general understanding of the other option available to you, in order to help you make an informed decision.

Deciding whether to consolidate your debts by declaring bankruptcy is a major financial decision; financial laws change from time to time and are different for country to country. If you are seriously considering these options make sure you speak to a qualified legal practitioner.

# Chapter 5

## How to Live Debt Free

If you have successfully paid off all your debts, congratulate yourself, you have accomplished something you should be proud of.

You now have one less thing to worry about and have the freedom to make decisions based on your hopes and aspirations rather than on your financial obligations.

You can now gain the thing you desire by working, investing and saving, rather than borrowing money and having fees and interest hold you back until the debt is paid.

Without debt, you now have the freedom to choose what you do with your money, and this freedom brings real peace of mind.

This is where the real fun and also the discipline begin.

All around us there is always something to we would like to buy and you will always be faced with creditors trying to push debt on you with new cards and incentives.

If you've just paid of all your debts and have achieved debt freedom you will know it's a lot easier to get into debt then it is to get out.

Now you have the opportunity to live a debt free life style.

In this chapter, I will be discussing steps you can take to live a debt free life style.

**Live a Frugal Lifestyle**

No matter how much you earn, it is still imperative to live within your means. Many people spend every cent they have because they cannot see past this week's activities. You don't have to feel like you're cheating yourself by living within your means.

Frugal living doesn't mean you have to go without. It means finding more affordable ways of doing things.

You can look wealthy while living frugal lifestyle. More affordable ways exist to house, clothe, feed and entertain yourself.

It is about mind-set and strategy rather than penance. You do this to achieve a financial objective. If you're young, it can be difficult to be frugal, most of you friends spend every cent they have, while you carefully make decisions to achieve financial dreams which seem so far away. Remember, you are responsible for your choices not theirs. A few years from now they will wish they had used their money more wisely.

**Try to Always Make Pragmatic Decisions**

When you feel the urge to buy something fancy, try to see if something cheaper can do the same job. For example if your car shopping and just need a car to get to work and back, ask yourself if you really need that luxury car you're tempted to buy or if a small more basic car is a better financial proposition.

## Fight the Compulsive Shopping Urge

Like almost any drug, excessive and impulsive shopping can be addictive.

You will find that most debt free people do very little shopping. When they go to the shops the usually buy what they need and come straight back out.

If you have uncontrolled shopping habits it's almost impossible to remain debt free-- compulsive shopping is an easy habit to get into.

## Look For Ways You Can Expand You Income

If you feel you don't earn enough to fund the kind of lifestyle you would like to have, you should think about finding more or new ways to earn money. Especially with today technology the opportunity are only limited by your imagination.

## Monitor Your Income and Expenses Frequently

One of the best ways to prevent excessive spending is to always be aware for your cash flow. People who live debt free usually know how much income they make and also know what their basic expenses are. This way they can adjust their expenses to create a better monthly budget.

Create a current financial statement like you did in chapter 3 and a realistic budget and stick to it.

## Ask For Help When You Need It

Even people who live debt free need help and advice from time to time.

Many People who live debt free become savvy about their finances because they consult with financial coaches or other such professionals.

Just be careful when taking advice, because when it comes to finances, free advice is usually worth what you pay for.

## Save When You Need to Buy Something Major

Debt free people usually don't take out loans when they need to fund major purchases. They think ahead and save for any expensive item they need.

They pay with cash, using money they have specially saved for that particular transaction; they patiently save and wait until they can afford that particular item.

## Take Personal Responsibility

Keep adding to your emergency fund so if you do experience any of life's surprises you are adequately prepared. People who are debt free are responsible enough to prepare for unexpected expenses.

For example if they lose their job they usually have enough money saved to last them at least three months.